Noah's Ark

Genesis 6-8

by Mary Manz Simon
Illustrated by Dennis Jones

SPIRIT PRESS

Read and Learn the Bible
LEVEL 1

See What God Made!

Noah's Ark

David and Goliath

Jonah and the Big Fish

The Good Samaritan

Too Tall, Too Small

Jesus Blesses the Children

Fishes and Loaves

Jesus Fills the Nets

© 1990 Concordia Publishing House

This edition published in 2004 by Spirit Press, an imprint of Dalmatian Press, LLC.
Used by permission. All rights reserved.

The SPIRIT PRESS name and logo are trademarks
of Dalmatian Press, LLC, Franklin, Tennessee 37067.
No part of this book may be reproduced or copied in any form
without the written permission of Concordia Publishing House.
ISBN: 140371-157-7
Printed in Canada
13772-1004

04   05   06   07   QSR   10   9   8   7   6   5   4   3   2   1

This Book Belongs to

_____

Name

_____

Date

To the Adult:

Early readers need two kinds of reading. They need to be read to, and they need to do their own reading. The *Read and Learn the Bible* series helps you to encourage your child with both kinds.

For example, your child might read this book as you sit together. Listen attentively. Assist gently, if needed. Encourage, be patient, and be very positive about your child's efforts.

Then perhaps you'd like to share the selected Bible story in an easy-to-understand translation or paraphrase.

Using both types of reading gives your child a chance to develop new skills and pride in reading. You share and support your child's excitement.

As a mother and a teacher, I anticipate the joy your child will feel in saying, "Hear me read a Bible story!"

Mary Manz Simon

And God said unto Noah . . . .
Make thee an ark of gopher wood.

GENESIS 6:13,14

Look at Noah.

Noah was God's helper.

God said to Noah,
"Make a boat.
Make a big boat."

"I promise I will send
    a big rain," said God.
Hurry, Noah! Hurry!

Drip, drop.

Hurry, Noah! Hurry!
Make a big boat.

Drip, drop.

Drip, drop.

Drip, drop, splash!

Noah was God's helper.

Drip, drop.
Drip, drop.
Drip, drop, splash!

Look at Noah make a boat.
Look at Noah make a big boat.

Drip, drop.

Drip, drop.

Drip, drop, splash!

Hurry, Noah! Hurry!
Splash, splash!

Look at the big boat.

Look at the big rain.

God said, "I promise
I will never send
such a big rain."

"Look," said Noah.

"Look at God's promise."

Read and Learn
25 words that tell the Bible story.

WORD LIST

a	was	make	will
I	boat	Noah	hurry
at	drip	rain	never
to	drop	said	helper
big	God's	send	splash
God	look	such	promise
the			

About the Author

Mary Manz Simon holds a doctoral degree in education with a specialty in early childhood education. She has taught at levels from preschool through post-graduate. Dr. Simon is the bestselling author of more than 40 children's books, including *Little Visits with Jesus*. She and her husband, the Reverend Henry A. Simon, are the parents of three children.